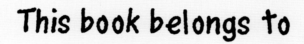

This book belongs to

Grandma Vah

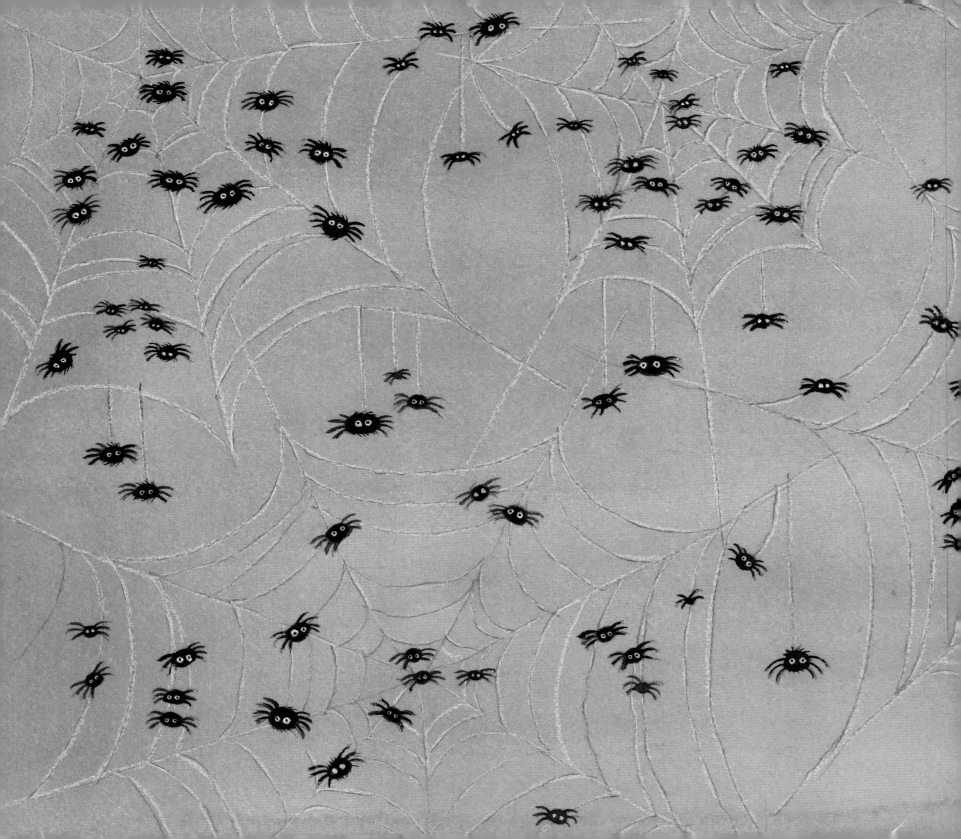

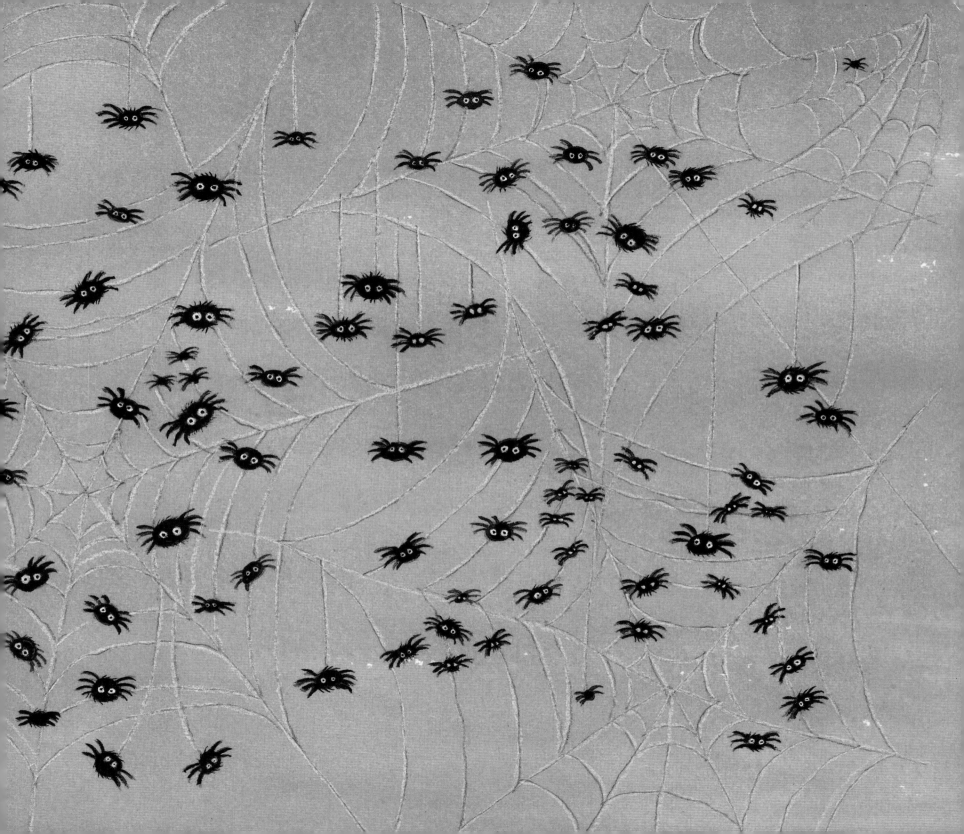

For the fearless Marlows:
Theo, Tegan, Billie, Alex, Guy, Milo
—LM

For Pruno, whose amazing stories would
scare away our childhood fears.
—JD

tiger tales

an imprint of ME Media, LLC · 202 Old Ridgefield Road, Wilton, CT 06897
This paperback edition published 2006
Originally published in the United States 2005
Originally published in Great Britain 2005
By Little Tiger Press, An imprint of Magi Publications
Text copyright © 2005 Layn Marlow; Illustrations copyright © 2005 Joelle Dreidemy

Library of Congress Cataloging-in-Publication Data

Marlow, Layn.
  The witch with a twitch / Layn Marlow, Joelle Dreidemy.
    p. cm.
  Originally published in Great Britain by Little Tiger Press, 2005.
  Summary: The other witches call Willa "cowardly custard," but when her beloved cat
is in real danger she has courage aplenty.
  ISBN-10: 1-58925-052-4 (hardcover)
  ISBN-13: 978-1-58925-052-9 (hardcover)
  ISBN-10: 1-58925-400-7 (paperback)
  ISBN-13: 978-1-58925-400-8 (paperback)
  [1. Witches—Fiction. 2. Cats—Fiction. 3. Courage—Fiction.] I. Dreidemy, Joelle, ill.
II. Title.
  PZ7.M34526Wit 2005
  [E]—dc22
                                                              2005007574

The Witch with a Twitch

by Layn Marlow

Illustrated by Joelle Dreidemy

tiger tales

Kitch was an ordinary witch's cat.
  But his beloved mistress, Willa, was
no ordinary witch.

The rest of the witches called her cowardly
custard, and even Kitch had to admit his witch
was a bit of a scaredycat.

Toads made her tremble,

nighttime made her nervous,

and spiders made her jump out of her skin!

Screech!

Willa was a very twitchy witch, which could only spell trouble for Kitch.

One dark night, Willa and
Kitch were zooming through
the sky on their broom.

Willa was already feeling twitchy in the darkness, when suddenly...

On no! An owl!
What a fright!
The witch twitched,
the broomstick pitched,

Aaaah!

and Kitch ended up in the mud!

Splat!

Poor Kitch!

Willa took him home for a special bath.
Using two drops of magic potion, she
began a spell to make Kitch's fur shiny and
sleek again. Drip, drip. But suddenly...

Oh no! A mouse!
What a terror!
The witch twitched,
the spell switched,

and Kitch found himself
covered in spots!
He looked ridiculous.

Squeak!
Squeak!

Poor spotted Kitch!

He spent the night trying to hide. But he was soon discovered by the other cats. They teased Kitch until he couldn't stand it anymore.

LOST
SWeeTY

please call
555-0123

He made up his mind
to run away to sea.

Dear Willa,
gone to be a
ship's cat.

Meanwhile, Willa searched all night
for the spell to cure Kitch.

Finally, she found it and hurried to help her spotted cat.

But all she spotted was his note.

Willa was very upset.

Kitch was gone! She had to find him!

Willa searched high and low,

but she couldn't find Kitch
anywhere . . .

until at last, she saw a tiny boat being
tossed around on the stormy sea.

On the deck was a sickly looking Kitch.
He was overjoyed to see Willa again!

The witch raised her wand to cast a
calming spell on the water, but suddenly...

a gigantic

WHALE rose out of the ocean!

What a shock!

The boat dipped
and Kitch slipped—
right into the deep, cold water!

SPLASH!

He had never been so afraid.
Kitch was in real danger!

Without the slightest twitch,
Willa dodged the whale,

braved the waves,

and hauled her
dear cat to safety.

Back home, Willa magicked the spots away and fussed over her cat until he felt better.

Now Willa didn't give two hoots about swooping owls, or snooping mice, or even scary spiders! Kitch was safe and sound and very proud of his own dear, kind, BRAVE witch.

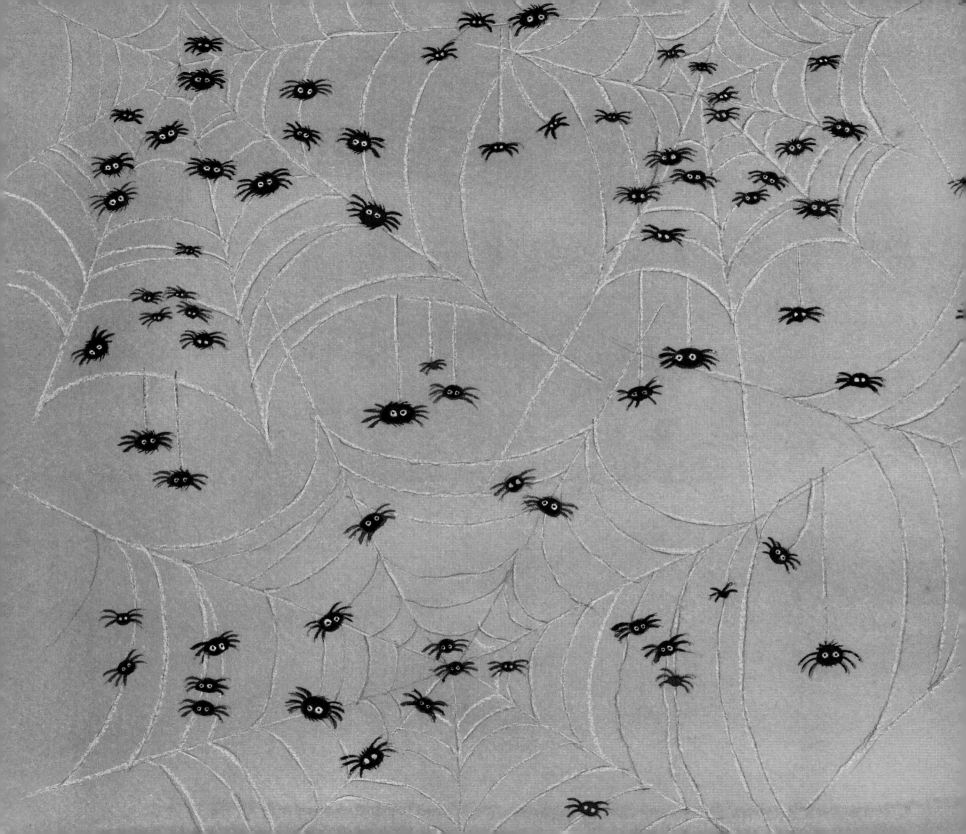

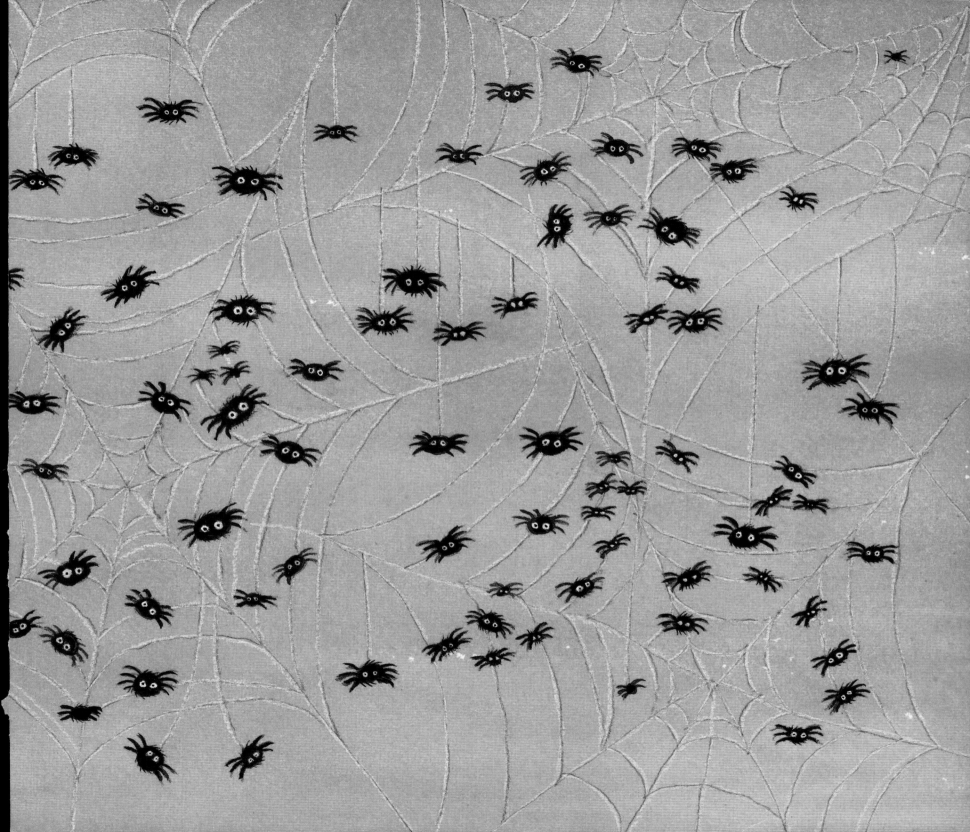

Where There's a Bear, There's Trouble!
by Michael Catchpool
illustrated by Vanessa Cabban
ISBN 1-58925-389-2

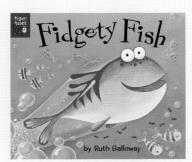

Fidgety Fish
by Ruth Galloway
ISBN 1-58925-377-9

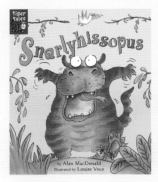

Snarlyhissopus
by Alan MacDonald
illustrated by Louise Voce
ISBN 1-58925-370-1

Night-Night, Emily!
by Claire Freedman
illustrated by Jane Massey
ISBN 1-58925-390-6

Explore the world of tiger tales!

More fun-filled and exciting stories await you!
Look for these titles and more at your local library or bookstore.
And have fun reading!

tiger tales

202 Old Ridgefield Road, Wilton, CT 06897

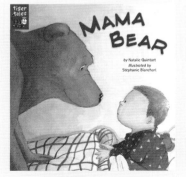

Mama Bear
by Natalie Quintart
illustrated by Stéphanie Blanchart
ISBN 1-58925-394-9

Gooseberry Goose
by Claire Freedman
illustrated by Vanessa Cabban
ISBN 1-58925-392-2

The Von Hamm Family:
Alex and the Tart
by Guido van Genechten
ISBN 1-58925-393-0

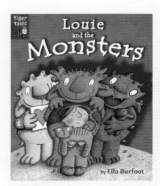

Louie and the Monsters
by Ella Burfoot
ISBN 1-58925-395-7